Unlocking the Secrets of Earning Online Income, from Passive Streams to Entrepreneurial Ventures

Chapter 1: The Digital Landscape: Understanding the Opportunities

Chapter 2: Building Your Online Presence: From Branding to Websites

Chapter 3: Monetizing Your Passion: Turning Hobbies into Profit

Chapter 4: Navigating E-Commerce: Selling Products and Services Online

Chapter 5: Unleashing the Power of Affiliate Marketing

Chapter 6: Harnessing the Potential of Dropshipping

Chapter 7: Freelancing: Maximizing Your Skills for Profit

Chapter 8: Creating and Selling Digital Products

Chapter 9: Mastering Content Creation: Blogging, Vlogging, and Beyond

Chapter 10: The World of Online Courses and Coaching

Chapter 11: Investing in Cryptocurrency and Other Digital Assets

Chapter 12: Building a Thriving Online Community

Chapter 13: Optimizing Your Online Presence for Search Engines

Chapter 14: Leveraging Social Media for Business Success

Chapter 15: Understanding and Utilizing Email Marketing

Chapter 16: Exploring the Realm of Influencer Marketing

Chapter 17: Overcoming Common Challenges and Pitfalls

Chapter 18: Scaling Your Online Business for Long-Term Success

Chapter 19: Staying Ahead in the Ever-Evolving Online Landscape

Chapter 20: Crafting Your Personalized Roadmap to Online Wealth

Chapter 21: Embracing the Power of Podcasting

Chapter 22: Exploring the World of Webinars and Virtual Events

Chapter 23: Diving Into Digital Advertising: PPC, Social Ads, and Beyond

Chapter 24: The Power of Outsourcing: Building a Virtual Team

Chapter 25: Building Your Personal Brand: Establishing Authority and Trust

Chapter 26: Exploring Alternative Revenue Streams: Membership Sites and Subscription Models

Chapter 27: The Future of Online Business: Trends and Predictions

Chapter 1: The Digital Landscape: Understanding the Opportunities

In this chapter, we embark on a journey through the vast and dynamic landscape of the digital world. We explore the unprecedented opportunities that the internet offers for individuals seeking to make money online. We delve into the evolution of the digital economy, from its humble beginnings to its current status as a powerhouse of economic activity. We examine the various sectors and industries that have flourished in the online realm, from e-commerce and affiliate marketing to freelancing and content creation. By gaining a comprehensive understanding of the digital landscape, readers will be equipped with the knowledge they need to navigate the complexities of the online marketplace and identify the most promising avenues for generating income.

Chapter 2: Building Your Online Presence: From Branding to Websites

In this chapter, we dive into the essential steps involved in establishing a strong and effective online presence. We explore the fundamentals of branding, emphasizing the importance of creating a cohesive and compelling identity that resonates with your target audience. We discuss the key elements of a successful website, from design and functionality to content and user experience. Readers will learn how to leverage various tools and platforms to build and optimize their online presence, ensuring that they stand out in a crowded digital landscape. By mastering the art of branding and website development, aspiring online entrepreneurs will lay the foundation for long-term success in the competitive world of online business.

Chapter 3: Monetizing Your Passion: Turning Hobbies into Profit

In this chapter, we explore the exciting opportunity to monetize your passions and interests by turning them into profitable online ventures. We discuss the importance of identifying your unique skills, talents, and interests and leveraging them to create value for others. Whether you're passionate about photography, cooking, fitness, or any other hobby, there are countless ways to monetize your expertise and creativity in the digital age. We provide practical tips and strategies for monetizing various hobbies, from selling handmade crafts and artwork to offering online courses and workshops. By harnessing the power of passion, readers will discover how to transform their hobbies into lucrative income streams that bring fulfillment and financial rewards.

Chapter 4: Navigating E-Commerce:

Selling Products and Services Online

In this chapter, we delve into the world of e-commerce and explore the opportunities and challenges of selling products and services online. We discuss the rapid growth of the e-commerce industry and its impact on traditional retail business models. From setting up an online store to managing inventory and processing payments, we provide practical guidance for aspiring e-commerce entrepreneurs. We explore the various e-commerce platforms available, from self-hosted solutions like Shopify and WooCommerce to third-party marketplaces like Amazon and eBay. Readers will learn how to effectively market their products and services online, attract customers, and drive sales. By mastering the intricacies of e-commerce, readers will be well-positioned to capitalize on the growing demand for online shopping and build a profitable online business.

Chapter 5: Unleashing the Power of Affiliate Marketing

In this chapter, we uncover the potential of affiliate marketing as a lucrative revenue stream for online entrepreneurs. We explain the concept of affiliate marketing and how it works, highlighting its benefits for both advertisers and publishers. Readers will learn how to become affiliate marketers and promote products and services from other companies in exchange for a commission on sales. We discuss the various affiliate marketing strategies and techniques, from content marketing and email campaigns to social media promotion and search engine optimization. By mastering the art of affiliate marketing, readers will gain access to a vast network of potential customers and partners, enabling them to generate passive income and grow their online business.

Chapter 6: Harnessing the Potential of Dropshipping

In this chapter, we explore the innovative business model of dropshipping and its potential for aspiring online entrepreneurs. We explain how dropshipping works, allowing entrepreneurs to sell products to customers without holding inventory or managing fulfillment. We discuss the advantages of dropshipping, including low startup costs, minimal risk, and the ability to scale quickly. Readers will learn how to set up a dropshipping business, find reliable suppliers, and select profitable products to sell. We provide practical tips for optimizing product listings, managing orders, and providing excellent customer service. By harnessing the potential of dropshipping, readers will discover a streamlined and cost-effective way to start and grow their online business.

Chapter 7: Freelancing: Maximizing Your Skills for Profit

In this chapter, we explore the world of freelancing and the opportunities it offers for individuals with valuable skills and expertise. We discuss the rise of the gig economy and the increasing demand for freelance services in fields such as writing, design, programming, and digital marketing. Readers will learn how to identify their marketable skills, create a compelling portfolio, and attract clients online. We provide practical advice for setting rates, negotiating contracts, and delivering high-quality work. Whether you're looking to supplement your income or pursue freelancing full-time, this chapter will equip you with the knowledge and tools you need to succeed in the competitive world of freelancing.

Chapter 8: Creating and Selling Digital Products

In this chapter, we explore the lucrative opportunity to create and sell digital products in the online marketplace. We discuss the various types of digital products available, from e-books and online courses to software and digital downloads. Readers will learn how to identify profitable niches, create high-quality digital products, and market them effectively to their target audience. We provide practical guidance for pricing digital products, protecting intellectual property, and delivering a great customer experience. By leveraging the power of digital products, readers will discover a scalable and passive income stream that has the potential to generate revenue for years to come.

Chapter 9: Mastering Content Creation:

Blogging, Vlogging, and Beyond

In this chapter, we delve into the world of content creation and explore the various mediums through which individuals can share their knowledge, expertise, and creativity with the world. We discuss the rise of blogging, vlogging, podcasting, and other forms of content creation, highlighting the opportunities they offer for building an audience and monetizing content. Readers will learn how to create compelling and engaging content, attract followers, and monetize their online presence through advertising, sponsorships, and other revenue streams. We provide practical tips for developing a content strategy, optimizing content for search engines, and maximizing engagement with your audience. By mastering the art of content creation, readers will unlock the potential to generate income while sharing their passion and expertise with others.

Chapter 10: The World of Online Courses and Coaching

In this chapter, we explore the booming market for online courses and coaching services and the opportunities it offers for individuals with valuable knowledge and expertise to share. We discuss the benefits of online learning and coaching, including convenience, accessibility, and flexibility. Readers will learn how to create and market their own online courses and coaching programs, from identifying a profitable niche to developing course content and pricing strategies. We provide practical advice for building a successful online course or coaching business, including tips for creating engaging course materials, attracting students, and delivering a great learning experience. By tapping into the growing demand for online education and coaching, readers will discover a rewarding and profitable way to share their skills and knowledge with others.

Chapter 11: Investing in Cryptocurrency and Other Digital Assets

In this chapter, we explore the exciting world of cryptocurrency and other digital assets and the potential they offer for generating wealth online. We discuss the fundamentals of cryptocurrency, blockchain technology, and other digital assets, highlighting their disruptive potential and the opportunities they present for investors. Readers will learn how to buy, sell, and trade cryptocurrencies, as well as how to identify promising investment opportunities and mitigate risks. We provide practical guidance for developing an investment strategy, managing a diversified portfolio, and staying informed about the latest developments in the cryptocurrency market. Whether you're a seasoned investor or new to the world of digital assets, this chapter will provide you with the knowledge and tools you need to navigate this rapidly evolving landscape and capitalize on the potential of cryptocurrency and other digital assets.

Chapter 12: Building a Thriving Online Community

In this chapter, we explore the power of online communities and the opportunities they offer for building connections, fostering engagement, and driving business success. We discuss the benefits of building an online community, including increased brand loyalty, customer retention, and word-of-mouth marketing. Readers will learn how to create and nurture an online community around their brand, product, or area of interest, from choosing the right platform to engaging with members and fostering meaningful interactions. We provide practical tips for growing and monetizing an online community, including strategies for attracting new members, moderating discussions, and monetizing through memberships, sponsorships, and other revenue streams. By harnessing the power of community, readers will discover a powerful tool for building a loyal audience and driving business growth in the digital age.

Chapter 13: Optimizing Your Online Presence for Search Engines

In this chapter, we delve into the world of search engine optimization (SEO) and explore the strategies and techniques for optimizing your online presence to rank higher in search engine results. We discuss the importance of SEO for driving organic traffic to your website or online business and the impact it can have on your visibility, credibility, and ultimately, your bottom line. Readers will learn how search engines work, the factors that influence search rankings, and the best practices for optimizing their website and content for search engines. We provide practical guidance for conducting keyword research, optimizing on-page elements, and building high-quality backlinks to improve search visibility and drive targeted traffic to your site. By mastering the art of SEO, readers will be able to maximize their online visibility and attract more customers to their business.

Chapter 14: Leveraging Social Media for Business Success

In this chapter, we explore the role of social media in the modern business landscape and the opportunities it offers for building brand awareness, driving engagement, and generating leads and sales. We discuss the benefits of using social media for business, including its ability to reach a large and diverse audience, facilitate meaningful interactions, and build relationships with customers and followers. Readers will learn how to create and optimize social media profiles for their business, develop a content strategy that resonates with their audience, and leverage various social media platforms to achieve their business goals. We provide practical tips for creating engaging content, growing your social media following, and measuring the effectiveness of your social media efforts. By mastering the art of social media marketing, readers will be able to harness the power of social media to grow their business and achieve success in the digital age.

Chapter 15: Understanding and Utilizing Email Marketing

In this chapter, we delve into the world of email marketing and explore the strategies and techniques for leveraging this powerful tool to drive engagement, nurture leads, and increase sales. We discuss the benefits of email marketing for businesses, including its ability to deliver targeted messages directly to your audience's inbox, build trust and credibility, and generate a high return on investment. Readers will learn how to build and grow an email list, create compelling email campaigns that resonate with their audience, and measure the success of their email marketing efforts. We provide practical guidance for crafting effective subject lines, designing eye-catching email templates, and optimizing email content for maximum impact. By mastering the art of email marketing, readers will be able to unlock the full potential of this versatile tool and drive meaningful results for their business.

Chapter 16: Exploring the Realm of Influencer Marketing

In this chapter, we explore the growing trend of influencer marketing and the opportunities it offers for businesses to reach and engage with their target audience in a more authentic and meaningful way. We discuss the rise of social media influencers and the impact they can have on consumer behavior, brand perception, and purchase decisions. Readers will learn how to identify and collaborate with influencers who align with their brand values and target audience, develop effective influencer marketing campaigns, and measure the success of their efforts. We provide practical tips for building relationships with influencers, negotiating partnerships, and maximizing the impact of influencer marketing on their business. By harnessing the power of influencer marketing, readers will be able to amplify their brand message, increase brand awareness, and drive meaningful engagement with their target audience.

Chapter 17: Overcoming Common Challenges and Pitfalls

In this chapter, we address some of the common challenges and pitfalls that aspiring online entrepreneurs may encounter on their journey to success. We discuss the importance of resilience, perseverance, and a growth mindset in overcoming obstacles and achieving your goals. Readers will learn how to identify and overcome common challenges such as fear of failure, lack of motivation, and burnout, as well as practical strategies for staying focused, motivated, and productive. We provide guidance for managing time effectively, setting realistic goals, and seeking support from mentors, peers, and other resources. By recognizing and addressing common challenges early on, readers will be better equipped to navigate the ups and downs of the entrepreneurial journey and ultimately achieve success in their online ventures.

Chapter 18: Scaling Your Online Business for Long-Term Success

In this chapter, we explore the strategies and techniques for scaling your online business and achieving long-term success in the competitive world of online entrepreneurship. We discuss the importance of scalability, sustainability, and innovation in building a successful online business that can grow and evolve over time. Readers will learn how to identify opportunities for growth, develop a scalable business model, and expand their operations to reach new markets and customers. We provide practical guidance for hiring and managing employees, outsourcing tasks, and automating processes to streamline operations and maximize efficiency. By mastering the art of scaling, readers will be able to take their online business to the next level and achieve sustainable growth and profitability in the long run.

Chapter 19: Staying Ahead in the Ever-Evolving Online Landscape

In this chapter, we discuss the importance of staying ahead of the curve in the ever-evolving landscape of online business and digital marketing. We explore the latest trends and developments shaping the digital economy, from emerging technologies and consumer behaviors to changes in search engine algorithms and social media algorithms. Readers will learn how to stay informed about the latest trends and developments in their industry, adapt to changes in the competitive landscape, and position themselves for success in the digital age. We provide practical tips for staying ahead of the competition, including investing in ongoing education and training, networking with industry peers, and experimenting with new strategies and techniques. By staying proactive and adaptable, readers will be able to stay ahead of the curve and maintain a competitive edge in the fast-paced world of online business.

Chapter 20: Crafting Your Personalized Roadmap to Online Wealth

In the chapter, we bring together the knowledge and insights gained throughout this book to help readers craft their personalized roadmap to online wealth. We discuss the importance of setting clear goals, defining success on your own terms, and developing a strategic plan to achieve your objectives. Readers will learn how to identify their strengths, weaknesses, opportunities, and threats, and leverage them to create a sustainable and profitable online business. We provide practical guidance for developing a business plan, setting actionable goals, and implementing a step-by-step action plan to turn their vision into reality. By crafting a personalized roadmap to online wealth, readers will be empowered to take control of their financial future and create the life of their dreams in the digital age.

Chapter 21: Embracing the Power of Podcasting

In this chapter, we explore the rapidly growing medium of podcasting and its potential for entrepreneurs to reach and engage with their target audience in a unique and impactful way. We discuss the benefits of podcasting for businesses, including its ability to build authority, foster connections, and attract a loyal audience. Readers will learn how to start their own podcast, from choosing a niche and format to recording, editing, and publishing episodes. We provide practical tips for promoting a podcast, growing an audience, and monetizing through sponsorships, affiliate marketing, and other revenue streams. By embracing the power of podcasting, readers will discover a powerful tool for building their brand, connecting with their audience, and driving business growth in the digital age.

Chapter 22: Exploring the World of Webinars and Virtual Events

In this chapter, we dive into the world of webinars and virtual events and the opportunities they offer for businesses to educate, engage, and convert their audience online. We discuss the benefits of hosting webinars and virtual events, including their ability to generate leads, build relationships, and drive sales. Readers will learn how to plan, promote, and host successful webinars and virtual events, from choosing a topic and format to selecting the right platform and technology. We provide practical tips for delivering engaging presentations, maximizing audience participation, and measuring the success of your events. By exploring the world of webinars and virtual events, readers will discover a powerful tool for connecting with their audience, showcasing their expertise, and achieving their business goals in the digital age.

Chapter 23: Diving Into Digital Advertising: PPC, Social Ads, and Beyond

In this chapter, we delve into the world of digital advertising and explore the various platforms and strategies available for reaching and converting customers online. We discuss the benefits of digital advertising for businesses, including its ability to target specific audiences, track performance, and achieve measurable results. Readers will learn about the different types of digital advertising, including pay-per-click (PPC) advertising, social media advertising, display advertising, and native advertising. We provide practical guidance for creating and optimizing digital ad campaigns, from setting goals and defining target audiences to designing ad creatives and monitoring performance metrics. By diving into the world of digital advertising, readers will gain valuable insights into how to leverage this powerful tool to reach their business goals and maximize their return on investment.

Chapter 24: The Power of Outsourcing:

Building a Virtual Team

In this chapter, we explore the benefits of outsourcing and building a virtual team to support and scale your online business. We discuss the various tasks and roles that can be outsourced, from administrative tasks and customer service to content creation and marketing. Readers will learn how to identify tasks that can be outsourced, find and hire qualified freelancers and contractors, and manage a virtual team effectively. We provide practical guidance for setting expectations, communicating effectively, and ensuring accountability and productivity among team members. By harnessing the power of outsourcing, readers will be able to focus on their core strengths and priorities, while delegating tasks and responsibilities to qualified professionals who can help them achieve their business goals more efficiently.

Chapter 24: The Power of Outsourcing:

Building a Virtual Team

In this chapter, we explore the benefits of outsourcing and building a virtual team to support and scale your online business. We discuss the various tasks and roles that can be outsourced, from administrative tasks and customer service to content creation and marketing. Readers will learn how to identify tasks that can be outsourced, find and hire qualified freelancers and contractors, and manage a virtual team effectively. We provide practical guidance for setting expectations, communicating effectively, and ensuring accountability and productivity among team members. By harnessing the power of outsourcing, readers will be able to focus on their core strengths and priorities, while delegating tasks and responsibilities to qualified professionals who can help them achieve their business goals more efficiently.

Chapter 25: Building Your Personal Brand: Establishing Authority and Trust

In this chapter, we explore the importance of personal branding and its impact on building authority, trust, and credibility in the online marketplace. We discuss the benefits of personal branding for entrepreneurs, including its ability to differentiate yourself from the competition, attract opportunities, and command higher prices for your products and services. Readers will learn how to define their personal brand, identify their unique value proposition, and communicate their brand message effectively across various online channels. We provide practical tips for building a strong personal brand, including developing a consistent brand identity, creating valuable content, and engaging with your audience authentically. By building their personal brand, readers will be able to establish themselves as trusted authorities in their niche and attract more opportunities for growth and success in their online ventures.

Chapter 26: Exploring Alternative Revenue Streams: Membership Sites and Subscription Models

In this chapter, we explore alternative revenue streams such as membership sites and subscription models and their potential for creating recurring income streams and fostering long-term customer relationships. We discuss the benefits of membership sites and subscription models for businesses, including predictable revenue, increased customer lifetime value, and enhanced customer loyalty. Readers will learn how to create and launch a membership site or subscription-based offering, from defining membership tiers and pricing to delivering exclusive content and benefits to members. We provide practical guidance for attracting and retaining members, managing subscriptions, and optimizing the membership experience for maximum engagement and retention. By exploring alternative revenue streams, readers will discover new opportunities to monetize their expertise and content while providing ongoing value to their audience.

Chapter 27: The Future of Online Business: Trends and Predictions

In this final chapter, we peer into the future of online business and explore emerging trends, technologies, and opportunities that are shaping the digital economy. We discuss the evolving landscape of online business, from the rise of artificial intelligence and machine learning to the growing influence of augmented reality and virtual reality. Readers will gain insights into key trends and predictions that are likely to impact the future of online business, from the rise of voice search and conversational commerce to the growing importance of sustainability and ethical business practices. We provide practical guidance for staying ahead of the curve, adapting to change, and seizing opportunities as they arise. By exploring the future of online business, readers will be better prepared to navigate the challenges and opportunities that lie ahead and position themselves for success in the dynamic and ever-changing digital landscape.

Thank You for Reading "How To Make Money Online"!

We want to extend our sincerest gratitude for taking the time to read our ebook. We hope that you found it informative, inspiring, and actionable. Your commitment to learning and exploring new opportunities in the digital landscape is commendable, and we're thrilled to have been a part of your journey.

We understand that embarking on the path to making money online can be both exciting and challenging. That's why we crafted this ebook to provide you with comprehensive insights, practical strategies, and expert guidance to help you navigate the complexities of the online marketplace and achieve your financial goals.

As you move forward on your online entrepreneurial journey, remember that success is not just about making money—it's also about creating value, serving others, and making a positive impact in the world. Stay focused, stay motivated, and never stop learning and growing.

If you found this ebook helpful, we would greatly appreciate it if you could share it with your friends, family, or colleagues who might also benefit from the information. Additionally, don't hesitate to reach out to us with any questions, feedback, or success stories you'd like to share.

Once again, thank you for choosing to read "How To Make Money Online". We wish you all the best on your journey to online wealth and success!

Warm regards,

Lekh Narayan Tandekar & Laxni Kumbhkar
RB & LN TANDEKAR PUBLICATIONS

www.ingramcontent.com/pod-product-compliance
Lightning Source LLC
Chambersburg PA
CBHW040302220526
45473CB00002B/560